I'm So Ugly

(and other poems)

by

Jonkers

(www.writtenbyjonkers.co.uk)

Illustrated by

Henryk Jachimczyk

(www.henthepen.co.uk)

All rights reserved
Copyright © Jonkers, 2018

The right of Jonkers to be identified as the author of this
work has been asserted in accordance with Section 78
of the Copyright, Designs and Patents Act 1988

The book cover picture is copyright to Jonkers

This book is published by
Grosvenor House Publishing Ltd
Link House
140 The Broadway, Tolworth, Surrey, KT6 7HT.
www.grosvenorhousepublishing.co.uk

This book is sold subject to the conditions that it shall not, by way of
trade or otherwise, be lent, resold, hired out or otherwise circulated
without the author's or publisher's prior consent in any form of binding or
cover other than that in which it is published and
without a similar condition including this condition being imposed
on the subsequent purchaser.

A CIP record for this book
is available from the British Library

ISBN 978-1-78623-239-7

Also by Jonkers:

Jimpy

Jimpy 2 (Chaos and Cat-astrophe)

Terry Scope's Telescope

Dedicated to Janette (Mrs Jonkers) and Luke

My Mum

My Dad

With Love

Contents

1.	Shopping at the Zoo-permarket	1
2.	First Day at School	3
3.	Mickey Flynn	5
4.	I'm So Ugly	6
5.	Bunny	11
6.	Animal Mix Up	12
7.	The Small Boy	14
8.	Gassing With My Brother	16
9.	Halloween	18
10.	Girls Get Up My Nose	20
11.	Can a Crocodile Catch Chicken Pox?	23
12.	The Tortoise and the Hare	24
13.	A Little Cow	28
14.	I Thought That I Was Rooney	29
15.	The Summer Lake	30
16.	Bare, Naked Trees!	31
17.	How Old?	32
18.	Brotherly Love?	33
19.	Vegicide	35
20.	A Boring Old Fart	37
21.	Tests	39
22.	S.A.T's Revision	40
23.	5 A-Day	41

24.	Optimistic Fan	43
25.	Working at the Zoo	46
26.	Getting Smaller	47
27.	Special Talents	48
28.	I Sat on a Man with a Hat On	51
29.	Romy the Rascally Rabbit	52
30.	Predators and Prey	53
31.	I Could Have Been...	54
32.	Attacked by a Turkey	55
33.	The Supply Teacher	56
34.	Out For a Run	58

Shopping at the Zoo-permarket

A zebra called Deborah was trying on shoes
But Deborah the zebra forgot she had hooves

A lion called Simon had bought a gold chain
But Simon the lion got it caught in his mane

Then a rat, name of Matt, tried on a new hat
But Matt the rat's hat was grabbed by the cat

A shark they called Mark tried on a new shirt
But Mark the shark actually wanted a skirt

An eel named Neil had ordered a meal
But Neil the eel was attacked by a seal

A snake called Jake bought a coffee and tea
Jake the snake drank with a bald chimpanzee

A panda, Miranda, had concealer to buy
Cos Miranda the panda had got two black eyes

A young snail called Dale had no need for socks
So Dale the young snail bought a pair for the fox

Peter the Cheetah spotted something to buy
The cheetah called Peter bought a red-spotted tie

A gorilla called Cilla had tried on pyjamas
But Cilla the gorilla instead bought bananas

A guinea pig called Winifred tried to buy a new hutch
But Winifred the guinea pig found the hutch cost too much

A mole named Joel bought a spade at a bargain
So Joel the mole can dig holes in the garden

A slug called Doug was left down by the greens
But Doug the slug had left slime on the beans

A bear called Claire had plenty of money
So Claire the bear bought gallons of honey

A koala named Carla bought gel for her hair
But Carla, koala, needed gel for a bear

The blue whale called Gayle couldn't shop anymore
Cos Gayle the blue whale was too big for the store.

First Day at School

"Oh, don't you look smart!" Mummy uttered with pride
As she carefully adjusted his tie.
My little boy Henry, so grown up now,"
She smiled, with a tear in her eye.

Henry kissed Mummy, his bag on his back
Then he nervously stepped out the door
His very first day at a brand-new school
Little Henry was little no more.

His heart beat much faster
And he started to shake
As he saw hundreds of children
Outside the front gates.

He took a deep breath
And forced himself in
In just half an hour
The school bell will ring

He entered the class
And sat at a desk
He tried to be brave
And he puffed out his chest

The bell sounded so loud
Like a bomb in his head
And the thump of the footsteps
Just filled him with dread

Like stampeding ants
They burst into the room
Henry is silent
But he'll have to speak soon

He'll have to speak soon
Or he'll look a fool
Cos Henry (Mr Walters)
Is the new teacher at school!

Mickey Flynn

Mickey Flynn has a very long chin
Which points right down to the ground
It could cost you dear, if you get too near
When his head is moving around.

Mickey Flynn has a hairy chin
With a long, brown goatee beard.
He's tried with a razor and electric shaver
But it still looks rather weird.

When Mickey Flynn gets an itchy chin
He can't reach the end by himself.
So he just has to wait, in a terrible state
Until it's scratched by somebody else!

Mickey Flynn is proud of his chin
But he did feel a bit of a fool,
When the other day, he went out to play
And his chin burst his best friend's ball!

But Mickey Flynn's chin is a marvellous chin
That is famous near and far,
For his no-hands trick, where he manages to pick
Pickled onions out of a jar!

I'm So Ugly

I'm so ugly and fat
Said George the gorilla
As he looked at himself
In the bathroom mirror.

Look at my belly
If you think yours is big
Moaned Siamese Sam
The pot-bellied pig.

And look at my legs
So short and stumpy
I've got good reason
For looking this grumpy.

I wish I was shorter
Said Jenny Giraffe
My legs are so long
I can't fit in the bath.

I'M SO UGLY

And wherever I go
I keep bumping my head
Not to mention the problems
When buying a bed.

Oh, stop all your moaning
For goodness sake!
At least you've got legs
Hissed Slippy the snake.

I have to spend all day
Flat on my belly
I can't even reach up
To turn on the telly.

Better to be flat
Than to carry these lumps
Moaned Colin the camel
With the two massive humps.

And look at my lips
And ridiculous teeth
My whole mouth turns sideways
Whenever I eat.

At least you can chew things
I just peck with a beak
And I can't even smile
Moaned Pete Parakeet.

I'd love to have either
A beak or a nose
Groaned Elsie the elephant
With a trunk like a hose.

Instead of a beak
Try this in its place
Like a hoover's been stuck
On the front of your face.

And sorry to go on
But look at these things
They're meant to be ears
But they look more like wings.

Oh be quiet Dumbo!
You talk like a fool
Hooted Olly the owl
From the 'Wise Owl School'.

I've heard you all moaning
Now enough is enough
It's now my turn to speak
So give me some hush.

The animals were silent
No one made a noise
They knew they should listen
To the words of the wise.

I'M SO UGLY

He ruffled his feathers
And swivelled his head
The wise one was ready
And here's what he said.

Wrong colour
Wrong size
Big ears
Big eyes.
Wrong shape
Wrong height
Poor hearing
Poor sight.

Too fat
Too thin
Too wide
Too slim.

Too short
Too tall
Too big
Too small.

Too fast
Too slow
Too high
To low.

This is too short
And these are too long.
These just aren't right
And these are all wrong.

I wish I was this
And I wish I was that
Could fly like a bird
Or spring like a cat.
Was as fast as a cheetah
Or strong as an ox
As brave as a lion
Or sly as a fox
But I'm not!

The owl suddenly stopped
And gazed all around
As he scanned with his eyes
They made not a sound.

Like a pause from an actor
He bided his time
Before slowly beginning
The rest of his rhyme.

Once when thinking deeply
I asked Me and Myself
If they had ever wanted
To be anybody else.

Myself said no he hadn't
And Me said he agreed
Just be happy as you are
Said I, Myself and Me.

The speech was now ended
So stopped the wise old bird
While all the others puzzled
At the wisdom of his words.

Bunny

There is a young rabbit called Bunny
Who goes in the run when it's sunny
When it's time to come in
I try to grab him
But he bites me and thinks that it's funny!

Animal Mix-up

**The animals have been mixed up
And I'm afraid the verbs have too
Perhaps you could try to work some out
So they can all go back to the zoo.**

The monkodile was snozing in the sun
While the octolope sprimped on the land.
A buffagator snowled very loudly
And a rattlerus splithered on sand.

The badgalo trambled towards the bank
As a giroceros drurped from the pool.
And some camkeys swundled overhead
While the antephins sprived to keep cool.

The fricklebacks darped in the rushes
As the snager slinced a way through the reeds.
And a terrible terrabil scambled by
As the chimpsters swittled up trees.

I'M SO UGLY

A tougaroo flounced quickly past
As a butterbit clambled up high
And a group of snorse galloted forward
As a pandotamus plaggered by.

A tortipede waffled slowly past
As a crocoros gnapped on some roots
Some newpoles surflicked in the pond
As the hippoffe gratched for some shoots.

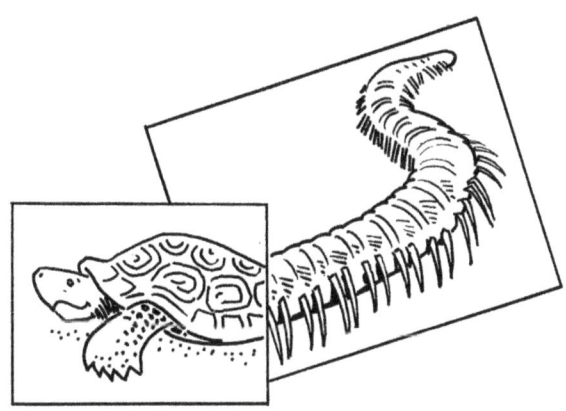

**So how many animals did you find?
And were there some verbs that you found?
Because I'm afraid if you didn't find any
Then this zoo will be forced to shut down.**

The Small Boy

There is a boy in my class
Who isn't very tall
In fact, if I am honest
I have to say he's small.

His feet come nowhere near the ground
When he sits down on his chair
His little legs and tiny feet
Just dangle in the air.

He isn't good at football
And he isn't very quick
He's really bad at hockey
'cause he's shorter than the stick

He said to me the other day,
"I wish I wasn't small
I'm sure I would be happier
If I was six feet tall."

"I guess we could try stretching you,"
I mischievously said
So I grabbed him by the ankles
And BIG DAVE grabbed his head

He made some dreadful noises
As we pulled with all our strength
Was this really working?
Had he really gained in length?

We both tugged even harder
But then we heard a crack
Dave had pulled his head off
And couldn't push it back

I'M SO UGLY

The teacher then came in the room
And gasped in total fright
He almost toppled over
So shocking was the sight

He looked at Dave, he looked at me
He knew my reputation
He stared at me and asked me for
Some kind of explanation

"I pretended we could stretch him sir
But then he lost his head
I wasn't trying to hurt him sir
I was just 'pulling his leg'!"

There was a boy in my class…

Gassing with my brother

I'm not sure what the rules are
And I don't know how it started
But I reckon it's when one of us
(Probably him) had farted

Now most nights, when the lights are out
The competition starts
But do we judge the sound or smell
Of our glorious, full-on farts?

He goes first, then I respond
Then he brews up yet another
We continue trading blow offs
As we try to gas each other

I hear my brother giggling
Just when I thought he'd stopped
A 'silent but deadly' waft of gas
Has been secretively dropped

I know the stench is coming
Wafted over by my brother
So I take a breath, hold my nose
And hide beneath the covers

I still hear my brother chuckling
No doubt he's feeling proud
But then I drop a thunder clap
He laughs, cos it's so loud

I'M SO UGLY

But then I don't know what to do
Should I stay beneath the covers?
And hope that my guff doesn't smell
As rotten as my brothers

I decide to shed the covers
Desperately hoping
That the smell may now have drifted off
Through the window mum left open

But no! The smell still lingers
I've made the wrong decision
And despite doing the loudest fart
I've lost the competition!

Halloween

With plastic fangs and rubber bats,
With scary masks and pointed hats
The children roam around the streets
Playing tricks and bagging treats.
A night for laughter, a night for fun,
But Halloween's not yet begun.
For when the children are safe in bed,
With pleasant dreams inside their heads,
Strange stirrings can be heard outside
As unnatural beings start to rise.
A gust disturbs the gentle breeze
As something swoops above the trees.
Silhouetted against the moon
Is seen a witch upon a broom.
With straggly hair and long black cloak
Then puff! Vanished in a cloud of smoke.
Another, cackling, whizzes by
Then disappears into the sky.
Wizards too begin appearing
To meet up in the forest clearing.
Where spells and potions will be brewed
And frog's and toad's eyes will be stewed.
The witches give the brew a mix,
Stirring with their wooden sticks.

I'M SO UGLY

With evil laughter and wicked smiles
They wait until the cauldron boils.
Then suddenly the spirits rise
And ghosts and spectres come alive,
Flying round the witches' heads,
Singing songs about the dead.
A gathering of Satan's choir,
Darkest black, with eyes of fire.
Round and round the spirits fly
Screeching out their dreadful cries.
Even the witches start to shake
So terrible is the noise they make.
Then suddenly they start to drop
And melt away back in the pot.
The witches quickly try a spell
To summon the spirits back from Hell,
But they have gone and won't be seen
Until next year, on Halloween.

Girls Get Up My Nose

When I was eight, I used to think
That girls were just annoying
Telling tales about the boys
Arguing and crying
(Carrie was the worst!)

I thought the same, when I was nine
That girls were just a pain
Giggly, silly, soppy things
Who drove the boys insane.
(Carrie was the silliest!)

At ten, things didn't change that much
They still got up my nose
Though some of them, like Millie
Were okay, I suppose.
(But not Carrie!)

At eleven years I'd changed a bit
But still thought girls were silly
Most of them were, anyway
But that's when I kissed Millie.
(I'd never kiss Carrie!)

At twelve, things were quite different
Though I still found most girls strange
My feelings towards a few of them
Had definitely changed.
(Carrie was still a strange one!)

I fell in love at thirteen
I fell in love with Millie
But when I told her, she just laughed
And said that I was silly.
(Carrie didn't laugh.)

I'M SO UGLY

From fourteen, through to fifteen
I pined for lovely Millie
Although she was now going out
With an older boy, called Billy
(Carrie comforted me.)

At sixteen, school was over
And we went our separate ways
Millie couldn't wait to leave
I was miserable for days.
(Carrie kissed and hugged me when we left.)

At seventeen it was college
A very different world
New life, new friends, new learning
And a difference mix of girls.
(Carrie stayed on at school.)

I fell in love with Laura
The same as me, eighteen
Intelligent and beautiful
A dazzling beauty queen.
(Carrie had moved away to Uni.)

At nineteen, still with Laura
The romance going strong
This one will last for ever
Nothing can go wrong.
(I hope Carrie is happy too.)

But suddenly at twenty
Something isn't right
Although we love each other
All we seem to do is fight
(I wish I could talk to someone.)

At twenty one, it's over
And again I'm on my own
Then one day, a familiar voice
Leaves a message on my phone.
(Carrie is back from Uni.)

At twenty two and twenty three
And then at twenty four
Me and Carrie become good friends
Friends but nothing more.
(Carrie's a great friend.)

At twenty five and twenty six
When alone I start to miss her
Then out the blue, next time we meet
I feel an urge to kiss her.
(Carrie is a close friend)

By twenty seven, things have changed
We're definitely not just friends
Love was maybe always there
And we got there in the end.
(Carrie and me together.)

At twenty eight, I'm now engaged
To that 'annoying', 'silly' Carrie
Who used to get right up my nose
And now I'm going to marry.
(Carrie doesn't annoy me any more -well not much!)

Now I'm almost thirty six
And our son is almost eight
He said he likes school mainly
It's just the girls he hates!
(Especially a girl called Maisie.)

Can a Crocodile Catch Chicken Pox?

Can a crocodile catch chicken pox?
Can a meerkat get bird flu?
Can a rabbit get mad cow disease?
Can a cat get swine flu too?

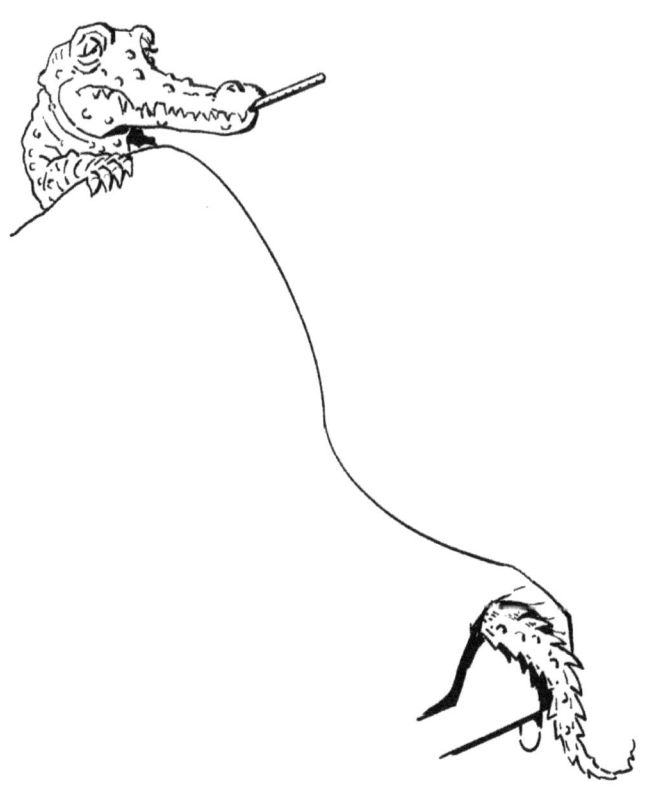

The Tortoise and the Hare

The tortoise slipped his Reeboks on
In preparation for the race.
He crouched down on the starting blocks,
Determination on his face.

The hare, still in his pyjamas,
Lay bathing in the summer sun,
So relaxed about the outcome
He didn't even hear the gun.

The tortoise with full alertness
Pushed the blocks with all his power
And sprinted off across the field
At almost one mile an hour.

I'M SO UGLY

The lazy hare opened his eyes
To see the tortoise trundle off.
'Be careful you're not caught speeding!'
The cruel hare began to scoff.

But the tortoise just ignored him
And maintained his steady pace,
Sensible, continual movement,
Those were his tactics for the race.

The hare at last began to change,
Pulling on his Adidas vest,
He ran a couple of metres
Then laid down for another rest.

Meanwhile, the tortoise ambled on,
With a slow but relentless pace,
He didn't care how he did it,
But he just had to win the race.

Meanwhile, the hare stood up again
And this time he started to run.
Not because he thought he'd lose the race,
He just wanted to have some fun.

And very soon he saw the shell
Of the tortoise up ahead.
He laughed as he drew beside him,
And these are the words he said.

'Just because Aesop's fables said
A tortoise had beaten a hare,
Unless you're slow in the mind as well
You must see that this race is not fair.'

'For I could beat you at a jog,
Or doing a flat-belly crawl,
To think you even have a chance
Just makes you a dim-witted fool.'

The tortoise still kept on walking,
Ignoring the hare's cruel jibes,
If he was to be defeated
He would lose with honour and pride.

The winning post was now in sight
And the hare continued to scoff,
He climbed onto the tortoise's shell
And challenged him to shake him off.

Despite the tortoise's efforts,
The hare just thanked him for the ride,
Until deciding to get down,
When he slid down the shell like a slide.

The hare pretended he'd hurt his leg,
As he hobbled towards the line,
Crying 'I think I've broken it!'
But yet laughing all of the time.

Then suddenly the laughing stopped,
As the hare doubled up in pain,
But the tortoise still ignored him
Convinced it was part of the game.

I'M SO UGLY

But the hare just kept on screaming,
As the finishing line was crossed,
By the proud and joyful tortoise.
Yes, the big-headed hare had lost.

For he'd been so busy mocking,
That the foolish, numb-brained hare
Hadn't looked where he was going
And had stepped right into a snare.

So the moral of this story
Is don't be boastful like the hare,
I'll leave it up to you to guess
If the tortoise released the snare.

A Little Cow

A little cow stood in a field
He looked down at his brother
Then he noticed something strange
His brother had an udder
He nudged his dad, the big old bull
And pointed at the udder
The bull just laughed
"You silly boy!
She's your sister, not your brother."

I thought that I was Rooney

I thought that I was Gareth Bale
Or even Harry Kane
I shot, the keeper saved it
Rebounded, missed again!

I thought that I was Neymar
I thought I was Defoe
I had a shot, but missed the ball
And almost broke my toe!

I thought that I was Suarez
Or Karim Benzema
I took a shot, but leaned right back
By miles it cleared the bar!

I thought I was Ronaldo
Or Van Persie, R.V.P
I sliced my shot, off for a throw
The ball lodged in a tree.

I thought that I was Messi
I thought that I was Rooney
I had a shot, my shorts fell down
I scored, and pulled a mooney!

The Summer Lake

The overhanging willow droops down,
Wilting in the breathless heat.
Lower boughs arch, to drape leaves
That bathe, refreshed in the cool water.

The sky's great canvas painted blue, clear
But for lightly dabbed patches of cotton-wool cumulus
That are burnt away to nothing as they dare
To move closer to the unremitting sun.

Blinding-white light reflects
From the lake's mirrored surface,
That is only rarely broken into ripples of
Shimmering fragments by a welcome breeze.

Nature herself slowed to slumbering pace:
A majestic swan glides effortlessly past
With just a nonchalant kick
Of its orange, flippered feet.

A surfacing rudd gulps for air
As a water boatman paddles slowly by.
Lethargic carp and bream roll lazily on top of the water
As they bask in the hazy glow of the golden orb.

Dragonflies flitter and shine in turquoise brilliance,
Some engaged in mid-air courting,
Deflecting and spiralling as wings collide,
And chasing playfully through reeds and rushes.

Only the merrily humming bees remain busy,
Buzzing in and out of the lily flowers
That are opened wide as though smiling
At the radiant splendour of the bright summer's day.

Bare, naked trees!

Leaves on the garden
Leaves on the shed
Leaves in the birdbath
Leaves on my head
Leaves they are everywhere
Except on the trees
The branches look naked
Without any leaves
I know that it's Autumn
And that's just what trees do
But this year I'm ready
I've ordered the glue
You may think it's silly
You may think it's wrong
But this year I'm going to
STICK THEM BACK ON!

How Old ?

My head says I am 26
My legs say 63
My aches and pains say 99
It's confusing, as you see.

My sense of humour's 10 years old
My hair says 54
So what age am I really?
Well, I don't count any more.

My brain is sometimes 21
But sometimes 85
My heart and lungs are getting old
But at least I'm still alive!

Brotherly Love?

Michael's brother mocked him again
"You really are a twit, with a pea for a brain!"
"But…"
"I can hardly believe you could be such a fool."
"Haven't they taught you anything at your school?"
"But…"
"And I have to say that you're a wimp as well."
"Ooh, don't hurt me or else I'll tell."
"But…"
"Don't 'but' in cos I've hardly got started."
"Your B.O smells like a rhinoceros has farted!"
"But…"
"Your head's so big it looks more like the moon."
"And you're more full of gas than a helium balloon."
"But…"
"Your ears stick out and your nose is massive too."
"You've got four eyes, where most boys just have two."
"But…"
I just don't know how you can be my brother."
"If I could, I'd swap you with another."
"Yeah, but…"
"Someone who was less ugly than you."
"And someone who was less annoying too."
"But…"
"And one more…"
"STOP! STOP! STOP!

"My grades at school are much higher than you."
"I'm on level 5 and you're much nearer 2."
"I'm not a wimp; you know that's a lie."
"I just don't fight back cos I know that you'd cry."
"If you say that I smell, then you do too."
"Cos I always bath straight after you."
"As for my head and my ears and my nose."
"I'm not going to argue about any of those."
"And I don't care if you say I'm as ugly as sin."
"Cos you're not just my brother, you're my identical twin!"

Vegicide

Murder! Murder! The beetroot is bleeding,
The cucumber's been sliced in two.
The potato's been stabbed; he looks pretty bad
And they've cut up the parsnips too.

Murder! Murder! The beetroot's still bleeding,
The celery's been pierced in the heart.
The garlic's just mush, he's been mercilessly crushed
And they're tearing the lettuce apart.

Murder! Murder! I can't stop the bleeding,
Now, the onion's been skinned and then chopped.
They've already cut off the tails of the beans,
Now they've started to hack off the tops.

Oh, Murder! Murder! The beetroot is dead!
And four of the carrots have been diced.
News just coming through; they've been thrown in the stew
With the leek who's been brutally sliced.

Murder! Murder! Help! Help!
I think that I may have been seen.
But they'll never catch me; I'm too quick you see.
Reporter: Reg Runner Bean!

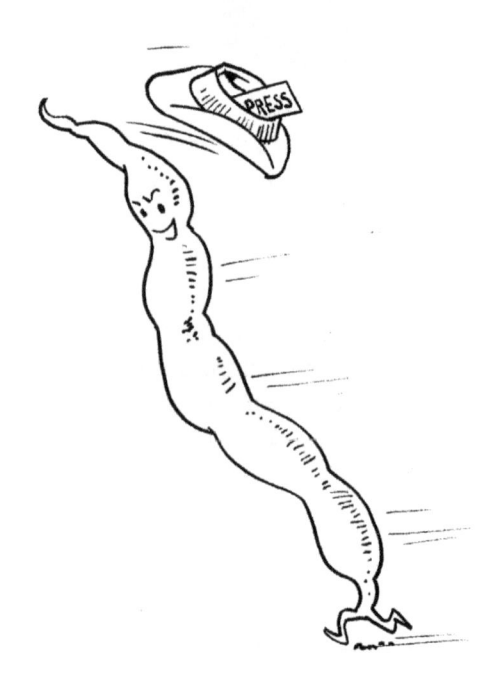

A Boring Old Fart

I don't own a Kindle
I just read a book
I don't watch the Bake Off
But yet, I can cook.

I've never tried tweeting
My phone isn't SMART
You may think of me
As a boring old fart.

I don't go on Facebook
It's a mystery to me
I don't have an Xbox
A DS or Wii

I don't download apps
I don't know what they are
A computer doesn't tell me
How to park my own car.

No Playstation 3
Or Mario Kart
You may think of me
As a boring old fart.

My watch tells the time
That's all it can do
An alarm doesn't tell me
When I need the loo.

When choosing a programme
I don't ask my TV
I just decide for myself
What I might want to see.

To remember a birthday
I don't ask my phone
I save it to the memory
In this brain that I own

Without all these gadgets
I've managed to survive
And according to my computer
I AM still alive!!

Tests

My favrit test is reading
I lick to read the best
The wun I reely hate tho
Is the stoopid spelling test!

SATS Revision

Tick, tick tick, ticking
The sound of cogs in heads
Slowly turning, grinding
SATS Reading revision

Click, click, click, clicking
Brains switched on
Serious, thinking mode
Reading test revision

Fiddle, fiddle, fiddling
With hair, with watch
Tapping pencils, chewing ends
Year 6 SATS revision

Shuffle, shuffle, shuffling
In seats, lean back
Close eyes, think, blink
SATS, year 6 revision

Panic, panic, panicking
Time! Look at clock
10 minutes – 3 pages
Reading test revision

Stop, stop, stopping
Breathe out, breathe in
Still silent, papers collected
End of Reading test revision

It's over – but
Please listen
After break
We start our Maths revision.

5 A Day

I know I should eat five a day
But I don't know what that means
Someone mentioned apples
Someone else said greens

Or is it 5 large chocolate bars?
Or 5 portions of chips?
Or 5 cream cakes, with icing on?
Or 5 big bags of crisps?

And what do 'greens' mean anyway?
Lots of things are green
Should I be eating frogs and grass?
Or bogies grilled or steamed?

Perhaps 5 scoops of ice cream
Covered in raspberry sauce
Washed down with 5 cans of coke
Non-diet ones of course!

Oranges are good for you
They give you vitamin C
So I'll eat 5 segments of chocolate orange
As dessert, after my tea.

I'll happily eat the apples
As long as they're covered in toffee
And I'll also drink plenty of water
But it will be mixed in with my coffee.

Should I eat 5 packets of biscuits?
And 5 bags of sweets every day?
Or 5 lumps of chocolate gateau?
Will that keep the doctor away?

So when you say have 5 a day
Please tell me what you really mean
And do baked beans count as double?
Cos they're orange, and they're beans?

Optimistic Fan

The season's nearly under way
The friendlies have been played
We're looking really strong this year
New signings have been made

By December we are bottom
But I think we'll still go up
And we're only in the second round
But I think we'll win the cup

But as the season carries on
Results don't go our way
And we're only three from bottom
On this, the final day

The final game – we need to win
Or else it's relegation
I know we'll win at least 3 – 0
And start a celebration

We're 2 0 down at half time
We've hardly touched the ball
We haven't had a shot yet,
We may only draw 2 all

Then half way through the second half
Our goalie whacks it forward
It bounces over their keeper
And amazingly we've scored.

And just ten minutes later
It's in the net again
A lucky *own* goal this time
We're right back in the game

But the clock says ninety minutes
And still we're only drawing
And now they're just defending
And it's hard to see us scoring

Desperately we pump it forward
Our striker fluffs his shot
But the defender stops it with his hand
The ref points to the spot!

Our number 10 steps forwards
Trying to stay cool
My own legs turn to jelly
As he stoops to place the ball

He gathers himself and takes a breath
It all comes down to this
The fans all pray together
Oh, please, oh please don't miss

He takes a steady run up
He looks to pick his spot
He hits the ball with power
A fierce, ferocious shot.

I'M SO UGLY

But he leant back when he hit it
And the football has been skied
We can hardly bare to watch it
As the ball goes high and wide

The whistle blows, it's over
The players are on the ground
And all around the stadium
The supporters make no sound

So we didn't win promotion
And we didn't win the cup
We went down to a lower league
But I'm sure we'll bounce back up

Cos I will never lose the faith
Though we've gone down a division
But don't say that I'm blinkered
Just admire my optimism!

Working at the zoo.

A girl got a job at the zoo
But wasn't quite sure what she'd do
Would she feed the big cats?
Or feed the snakes rats?
Oh no, she'd be sweeping up poo!

Getting Smaller

Why is the writing so small these days?
The printed words a foggy haze

It really does seem quite absurd
That books these days are always blurred

It's rapidly getting to the stage
Where it's just black marks upon a page

Like little ants just squashed together
And even 'Large Print's' not much better

It's not just books, what are they thinking?
Writing everywhere is shrinking

Writing can be hardly seen
On boxes, tubes, in magazines

Tiny instructions that once were clear
Are now so small, they disappear

I get dreadful headaches from constant squinting
As the words I read just keep on shrinking

I don't know why they've changed the size
For all it does is strain my eyes

But something else confuses me
It's really rather odd you see

Because even books I've read before
I can't read clearly anymore!

Special Talents

What has become of them?
What has happened to their special talents?
The local 'wheelie' champion
One hundred yards of perfect balance.

Wherever is the yoyo king
The best at 'walk the dog'?
Or the girl in my form, 7c
Who could imitate a frog?

Where is the expert stuntman
We nicknamed 'Crazy Mike'?
Who 'bunny-hopped' four house bricks
On his customised BMX bike.

What has happened to the Rubik's cube champ?
Or the hop-scotch number one?
The sports-day sack-race specialist
Who went faster than I could run!

I'M SO UGLY

Where is Tony Jackson now,
Who built the best go-karts?
And where is 'Puffing Billy'
The boy who lit his farts?

The space invaders high scorer?
The furthest jumper off the swing?
Where is the kid who was in the choir
But told to mime, not sing?

Where is the girl who laughed like a horse?
The boy who turned his eyelids inside out?
The girl who had double-jointed wrists?
The boy with the loudest shout?

Where is that disgusting boy
The champion bogey picker
Who also held the coveted title
Of champion bogey flicker?

What about the paper-folding
Origami queen?
Or the boy whose paper aeroplanes
Were the finest ever seen?

I hope they still remember
Cause it really would be sad
If just because they've now grown up
They've forgotten the talents they had.

I Sat on a Man With a Hat on.

I sat on a man with a hat on
The man had sat down on my chair
I sat on a man with a hat on
Cos I didn't know that he was there
I sat on a man with a hat on
So shocked, I jumped into the air
I sat on a man with a hat on
But still he stayed sat in my chair
So I sat on a man with a hat on
And squashed him, but I didn't care!

Romy the Rascally Rabbit

Romy was a rabbit
A rabbit in a run
A rascal of a rabbit
Thought escaping was such fun

He ran around the rabbit run
A rabbit in a rage
Riled and reckless Romy
Then lifted up the cage

This rascal of a rabbit
Ran round and round and round
Then grabbed the bottom of the cage
And wrenched it from the ground

The run was really rocking now
As he grabbed it with his teeth
Then raised the run right off the ground
And wriggled underneath!

And now he looks so innocent
That naughty flop-eared rabbit
As he sits in next doors garden
Nibbling on a carrot!

Predators and Prey

The cats are chasing dogs
The birds are chasing cats
The zebras chase the tigers
And the flies attack the bats

The mice are hunting eagles
The leopards flee from deer
The fish are biting crocodiles
The lions shake with fear

The rabbits hunt the foxes
The owls are chased by voles
The seals are hunting killer whales
The worms are after moles

The penguins hunt the polar bears
The wildebeest hunt cheetahs
Salmon attack the grizzly bears
And ants attack anteaters

Some animals are after *us*
They've begun attacking man
The rhinoceros, the elephant
The wild orangutan

Everything is changing
It's all been turned around
The prey are now the predators
Nature's upside down!

I could have been...

Hailed as the greatest living poet
Proclaimed as the master of rhyme
No one would match my brilliant verse
If only I had the time.

My very first novel would be number one
In the Literary critic's chart
A guaranteed best seller
But I haven't had chance to start.

A platinum disc would hang on my wall
A month after my debut release
But to compose this musical masterpiece
Would take me an hour at least!

So how about using the power and strength
Of my body instead of my brain?
Gold medallist and world champion athlete
But when am I going to train?

The first space explorer to travel to Mars
In a rocket I built by myself
But that planet is light years away from the Earth
So I decided to do something else.

Now, being gifted with so many talents
Which to use I just couldn't decide
So I never did anything really
But I could have done if I had tried!

Attacked by a Turkey

Gobble, gobble
Gobble, gobble
Peck, peck, gobble
GO AWAY!

Peck, peck
Gobble, gobble
Gobble, peck, gobble
LEAVE ME ALONE!

Gobble, gobble
Peck, peck
Peck, peck, peck
OUCH!

I kick at the turkey but miss
His gobble becomes a strange hiss
He's angrier now than before
I shout, but he just pecks me more!

He pecks at my ankle and leg
Bashing away with his head
He jabs me again and again
Causing me terrible pain

Gobble, gobble, peck, peck
I could almost ring his flippin' neck
Then I smile as I remember
What will happen in late December!

The Supply Teacher

Here he comes
Grey hair and beard
Why are supply teachers
Always so weird?

What's he looking at?
The strange-looking geek!
He's just standing there staring
Is he going to speak?

He looks really frightened
And we're only year five
Does he think we'll attack him?
Or skin him alive?

At last he does something
He's clapping his hands
To get attention (I think)
But no-one understands

They just keep on talking
Ignoring his clapping
He'll have to do better
Or we'll just keep on chatting

"Right, now sit down and listen,
It's register time."
He repeats it again
At least seven times

But still we're all talking
Now he's started to shout
But the kids hardly notice
And still mess about

I'M SO UGLY

He's getting more desperate
He's got fear in his eyes
Nothing is working
Whatever he tries

The noise just gets louder
And they pretend he's not there
So he's wasting his time
With that 'strict teacher's stare'

He thinks of escaping
He stares at the door
He can't believe this lot
Are worse than year four

He takes a deep breath
And shouts once again
But I'm afraid that the outcome's
Exactly the same

I almost feel sorry for him
But then I think, why?
He's a teacher after all
And worse, he's supply!

Out for a run

Warming and stretching
Warming and flexing
Stretching and flexing
Flexing and warming
Walking and jogging
Jogging and jogging
Jogging and jogging
Jogging and running
Jogging and jogging
Jogging and running
jogging and running
Running and running
Running and running
Jogging and running
Running and sweating
Huffing and puffing
Running and running
Running and running
Huffing and puffing
Sweating and running
Jogging and jogging
jogging and gasping
Gasping and jogging
Panting and puffing
Jogging and jogging
Jogging and jogging
Running and breathing
Sweating and running
Running and sweating
Running and running
Running and running
Running and jogging
Jogging and jogging

I'M SO UGLY

Jogging and jogging
Puffing and jogging
Puffing and jogging
Running and running and running
Sprinting and sprinting and sprinting and sprinting and…
Gasping and puffing
Gasping and puffing
Sweating and gasping
Sweating, sweating
Breathing, Breathing
Breathing, calming
Breathing
Stretch
Cool
Drink
Cool
Drink
Relax
Drink
Relax…and breathe.